Shepherd Blessings

Uplifting Insights from the 23rd Psalm

JIM BAILIFF

Copyright @2021 by James Bailiff

All rights reserved. No part of this book may be reproduced in any form or by any electronic or mechanical means, including information storage and retrieval systems, without permission in writing from the publisher, except by reviewers, who may quote brief passages in a review.

This publication contains the opinions and ideas of its author. It is intended to provide helpful and informative material on the subjects addressed in the publication. The author and publisher specifically disclaim all responsibility for any liability, loss or risk, personal or otherwise, which is incurred as a consequence, directly or indirectly, of the use and application of any of the contents of this book.

WORKBOOK PRESS LLC
187 E Warm Springs Rd,
Suite B285, Las Vegas, NV 89119, USA

Website:	https://workbookpress.com/
Hotline:	1-888-818-4856
Email:	admin@workbookpress.com

Ordering Information:
Quantity sales. Special discounts are available on quantity purchases by corporations, associations, and others.
For details, contact the publisher at the address above.

ISBN-13:	978-1-955459-59-4 (Paperback Version)
	978-1-955459-58-7 (Digital Version)

REV. DATE: 04/01/2021

SHEPHERD BLESSINGS:
Uplifting Insights from the 23rd Psalm

James D. Bailiff, Author

Dedicated to my
two beloved grandmothers
Lou Heaton and Alice Bailiff,
teachers by example

Shepherd Blessings

TABLE OF CONTENTS

Preface..pp. *i*

Chapter 1   The Shepherd's Nurturing Care   pp. *01*

Chapter 2   The Shepherd's Protective Care   pp. *14*

Chapter 3   The Shepherd's Protective Care   pp. *46*

Conclusion..pp. *57*

Notes...pp. *61*

James Bailiff

PREFACE

Since childhood, my attention was drawn to Psalm 23. Its appeal has continued through the stages and years of my life, speaking to my head and heart both in those times when my spirit was low in the valley and those in which it was high on the mountain. The psalm has a timeless, universal quality that places it among the world's most significant and meaningful literature.

The Psalter in which the psalm is contained is distinctive in that it has been responsibly described not as God's word to humans but, rather, humans addressing themselves to God both in praise and complaint.

Recognizing the deep wells of inspiration therein, the Jewish community gave the Psalter a sense of reverence and usage to merit it a place in the Old Testament, elevating it to the honored place of Scripture as early as the third or second centuries before the Christian era; well before the official canonization of the Old Testament at Jamnia in 90 AD.

So, Psalm 23 is the focus of my writing here in which I have attempted to analyze its message and consider its insights regarding the blessings that grow out of acknowledging the Lord as our Shepherd.

As I have indicated, there is something about this psalm that grasped my heart early on and has refused to loosen its grip. As a result, I have wanted to delve into it more intentionally. Given the instability with which we are surrounded--particularly during the last year filled with political chaos and a threatening pandemic (Covid-19), I have felt compelled to write, attempting to explicate the relevance of the psalm's insights and inspiration and to describe its fulfilling effects upon my life; hence the title Shepherd Blessings.

I am impressed with the way in which the psalmist pictures the writer's relationship with God as that of a sheep to its faithful shepherd, and with how faithful the shepherd is in nourishing, protecting and guiding its own. In that context he makes the shepherd/sheep relationship very personal, moving to describe it in intimate one-to-one terms that make clear the resulting influences upon his quality of life.

Depicting his life as a treacherous—though fulfilling and purposeful journey toward a glorious destination—the writer of the psalm talks about how the Lord shepherds him through threatening perils, nurturing and protecting him in such a way that he not only survives but thrives, both during the journey and at the point of its ending. Hence, the psalm is a virtual hymn of praise to the Lord for his glorious shepherding role which covers the span of his life.

Because the psalm comes to us from a pre-Christian culture, it does not utilize distinctive Christian imagery and terms. However, down through the ages, Christians have sensed that it lays a very meaningful groundwork for understanding the nature of Christ's shepherding role in our lives. It's as though the psalm anticipates the role Jesus will play with the Twelve and with all who dare to follow him then and now.

By declaring that the psalm anticipates the shepherding role of Jesus, I do not mean to imply that it sees the coming of the historical Jesus, specifically. Moreover, I do not have a sufficient understanding of the level at which the psalmist's messianic concept operated. In other words, I cannot, with theological competence, comment on whether he possessed a strong messianic consciousness or whether he actually expected an individual messiah. What I do mean with a reference to the psalm's anticipation is its affirmation of God's shepherding role in such a way that, when Jesus arrived on the scene, at least a couple of centuries later, he was able to fit, naturally and smoothly, into that role; apparently, both in his self-understanding and in the understanding of those who followed him.

In my writing, therefore, you will feel my swing, back and forth, between references to the psalmist's shepherd, Yahweh, and the incarnate form of Yahweh, Jesus. I affirm that, because his experience of God's shepherding and our Christian experience of it are very similar, yet distinct in some ways, the dynamic seems compatible and comfortable.

Perhaps our relationship with Jesus, whom we know as the Good Shepherd, is a bit more personal, given his human face, tender voice and gentle heart—all of which convey the essential nature of God—but God, for both the psalmist and for us, is the same.

However, there are important distinctions in the psalmist's understanding of human destiny and that of Jesus' followers. For example, the concluding verse of the psalm, *"...and I shall dwell in the house of the Lord my whole life long,"* suggests that the duration of the shepherd/sheep relationship is limited to the span of our earthly existence. On the other hand, Christians have tended to view the relationship as extending into life after death, i.e., for eternity. I will say more about this distinction at the appropriate point in this writing.

In short, it seems that the writer of Psalm 23 dramatically introduces the concept of the Lord's shepherding, a concept that Jesus will later take upon himself, personally becoming the Good Shepherd and, thereby, adding both beauty and meaning to the shepherding image.

As we position ourselves for delving into the psalm, please allow me a word to prepare us for its introductory verse which is loaded with significant implications that enhance our ability to find and experience its meaning. Three of these seem particularly important:

(1) There Are Some Keys to Understanding the Shepherding Concept

(2) Human Beings Need Guidance

(3) There Is a Need for of Caution in Choosing a Shepherd

1. There Are Some Keys to Understanding the Shepherding Concept

Most everyone knows about sheep and shepherds. Certainly, those familiar with biblical times are aware that they are visible throughout the Bible. In the agrarian societies of biblical times sheep were a prized commodity. So were shepherds who had the responsibility of overseeing them.

When the psalmist chooses to represent his life as that of a sheep, along with the Lord's shepherding oversight, he utilizes metaphorical figures, highly recognizable and clearly understandable to his readers or hearers.

Significantly, when Jesus came onto the scene centuries later, he chose these same metaphors to illustrate both the relationship he had with his followers and the dependability with which he fulfilled that relationship. To emphasize those relational dimensions, he expanded the imagery to that of "...*the good shepherd (who) lays down his* life for the sheep" (John 10:11—NRSV).

Solidly, therefore, in the Judeo-Christian tradition this Shepherd/sheep metaphor is established as a tool of communicating the quality of the relationship between the Lord and those who follow him faithfully.

Does this imagery imply that those who follow God's leading are, like sheep, naïve simpletons? Of course not! Neither the psalmist nor Jesus is suggesting such a negative image for people of faith. However, the metaphor does intend to convey the idea that our relationship with the divine is one in which we experience a subordinate role to that of our Shepherd. That subordinate position, however, is an enviable one for it is rooted in love that flows from both parties, love which, from our end, takes the form of faithful obedience to the Shepherd and, from the Shepherd's end, takes the form of loving commitment to the followers that enables us, through the shepherd's guidance and nurture, to reach our intended destinations.

In short, the relationship between sheep and shepherd is not to be construed in the negative terms of power-playing captivity and abuse, but in terms of loving community, filled with purposeful discipleship, journeying toward something good and beautiful for all creation.

2. Human Beings Need Guidance

With its imagery of sheep and shepherd, Psalm 23 defies the notion that human beings are autonomous or that God is non-directive. It acknowledges the conviction that, left to ourselves attempts at building our lives may create confusion and chaos. Hence the need for a strong shepherd to help us in the management of our affairs.

The writer of this psalm acknowledges that his life has found fulfillment precisely because, in his need for such, he has chosen to follow the leading of God. He seems to know that, by our nature, we humans have a pronounced need for a divine shepherd.

I share with you an incident from my own life that led me to a similar conviction of my need for guidance. The year was 1958 and our graduating seniors—including me—had gathered for our college baccalaureate service whose preacher was the late Reverend. Dr. John Paul Jones. As he rose to deliver his sermon, I found myself full of anticipation to receive his words. Clearly, I remember his announcement of the scripture text, Psalm 127:1-2 (King James Version), which reads as follows:

Unless the Lord builds the house, those who build it labor in vain. Unless the Lord watches over the city, the watchman stays awake in vain. It is in vain that your rise up early and go late to rest, eating the bread of anxious toil: for he gives to his beloved sleep.

Having chosen, during early adolescence, to turn

my life over to the Lord, I had already begun the process of building it. But, on hearing this scripture for the first time, abruptly, I became aware of my need, more intentionally, to invite God into the building process. With this refreshing experience, I seemed to hear, more clearly, the message that I can't do this on my own, that I need the Good Shepherd's guidance; that every human being does.

The psalmist seems to experience a similar need in his own life. Thus, out of his felt need, he turns outwardly toward a Divine Compass.

I have a daughter who works in the field of addiction therapy. Among her clients are persons who represent every kind of addiction imaginable. She holds the conviction that an addictive person begins the healing process when he or she recognizes that they have a problem and are in need of help.

As I reflect upon some 50 years of pastoral ministry, I am more convinced than ever that, in every human, there is an acute need for help in order to live abundantly. To all of us this insight should be self-evident: We all need divine shepherding!

3. There is a Need for Caution in Choosing a Shepherd

"The Lord is my shepherd...." By the time this psalm was written, the Jewish community had moved beyond its earlier stages in which it acknowledged

the existence of other gods [henotheism] (Exodus 15:11, Deuteronomy 32:8) onto solid belief in one God [monotheism]. So, the psalm begins with the declaration, *"The **Lord** is my Shepherd...."* As I read that, I remember the days of henotheism and imagine the psalmist surveying multiple divine options and settling on a conviction, born from experience, that he was choosing Yahweh (the Lord) and standing firm with that choice, and—again in my imagination—along with Joshua of old, he confronts us with a need to *"Choose this day whom you will serve...but as for me and my house, we will serve the Lord" (Joshua 24:15—King James Version).*

So, after what I imagine to be a process of careful discernment, the psalmist introduces the psalm with his decision: "The Lord is my shepherd...," not the gods of other regions and cultures, but Jehovah God!

If this is, in fact, the process followed by the psalmist, I experience his declaration as somewhat polemical, i.e., an expression of confidence in and praise to God as superior to any other shepherding option; yet is comes across to me as devotionally testimonial rather than argumentative.

What can we draw from the declaration? Given our contemporary context in which there are multiple "gods" offering themselves to deliver us, i.e., to lead us to fulfillment of life, aren't we compelled to exercise care and discretion in choosing the one who is able to help us succeed on that journey?

We can name some of those gods—materialism, humanism, nationalism, racism, sexism—each of which has its particular set of promises. Yet, as a Christian, I am compelled, as was the psalmist, to make a choice. I choose Jesus Christ to be my shepherd, in the process of which, incidentally, I learn that he has already chosen me.

Having identified the Lord as his shepherd, the psalmist is now ready to continue with his psalm of praise, stating, at the outset, that because the Lord is his shepherd, he will experience no lack of the things needed to make life full, meaningful and purposeful; thus, he declares, *"The Lord is my shepherd, I shall not want...."* (New Revised Standard Version)

In the chapters that follow I write about the astounding blessings that constitute the results of entering into a shepherding relationship with God; utilizing three chapters with these headings:

Chapter One

The Shepherd's Nurturing Care

Chapter Two

The Shepherd's Protective Care

Chapter Three

The Shepherd's Victorious Care

CHAPTER 1
The Shepherd's *Nurturing* Care

"The Lord is my shepherd, I shall not want (lack)."

The Lord's shepherding care comes in several forms including that of *nurture*. As surely as a flock of sheep is dependent upon their shepherd to lead them to sources that can nurture their well-being, this is the case for those who follow the Lord.

This is an insight that is frequently misunderstood by those without a faith orientation, whose number seems to be increasing. For example, at this point in the 21st century, the number of persons who list their religious preference as *none* is growing. I think this does not mean that all of the "nones" are faithless people, for I know a number of them who consider themselves to have abandoned *religious institutionalism* but not God. Obviously, however, such is not the case with all the "nones." There are those, of course, who, without any evident experience with the Divine, have concluded that either the Divine does not exist or that the Divine is not useful and relevant to their lives. It seems that they march to a different drumbeat than that of faith. To me, they appear to have given themselves to one of the most popular options in modern society, namely, *secularism*. Wrapped in its arms, they discard the need for an experience of transcendence designed to lift us out of a one-dimensioned, mundane flatness, choosing to believe that secularism is sufficient for their happiness.

In their book, *Longing for God,* Richard Foster and Gayle Beebe make a helpful descriptive distinction between persons walking on or searching for the path of faith in contrast with the character of society at large:

> Success or failure in the eyes of society is measured in terms of wealth, power, prestige and personal achievement. But success in the spiritual life is measured in terms of our ability to understand and address our own spiritual condition as well as the spiritual needs of others. Yet there is almost nothing in our contemporary culture that directs us this way. **1**

With Psalm 23's emphasis upon "right paths" echoing in the background, I agree with Foster's and Beebe's conclusion that contemporary society offers us, not *right* paths but *wrong* ones, those that lead us to believe we can be fulfilled without opening ourselves to the leading offered by the Good Shepherd.

This is not to suggest that we cannot achieve and accomplish apart from faith. However, it is to emphasize that the "restoration of our souls," which follows upon God's nurturing acts which Psalm 23 describes (verses 2-3) and the gift of the "abundant life" which was the purpose of Jesus' coming as our "Good Shepherd" (John 10:10), are foundational for a truly happy and purposeful living. Again, hear Foster and Beebe:

> We can be successful by all the conventional measures of society and still be clinically unhappy. We are unhappy because the life we live is unbalanced and we cannot give ourselves to the priorities and relationships that form the foundations of a meaningful life. We give ourselves instead to misplaced priorities and superficial relationships because we believe that if we just earn a lot more money or gain a little more respect, we will achieve the inner peace we long for and seek.
>
> To discover a life of balance is to find the true source of happiness in God. It is to know that our life must connect with God if we are to engage in activities that bring ultimate meaning to our existence. **2**

Affirming, then, that the life of faith offers us a positive pathway to discovering our essential meaning and purpose, and therefore, the *abundant life*, let us return with our focus upon the insights offered by Psalm 23 regarding nurture.

Beautifully, the psalm describes the Good Shepherd's nurturing activity:

"He makes me lie down in green pastures; he leads me beside still waters; he restores my soul" (vss. 2-3a-New Revised Standard Version [NRSV]). Other translations/paraphrases add clarification. For example, *"He lets me rest in fields of green grass and leads me to quiet pools of fresh waters" (TEV)* or *"In green meadows he will make me lie down; near tranquil waters will he guide me, to refresh my being"* (Anchor Bible).

Now, let's dig a little deeper into the verses of the psalm's opening passage in order to absorb more about the scope of the Good Shepherd's nurturing ministry.

Initially, we are given the image of *"green pastures."* Can you imagine a hungry flock of sheep with their shepherd, approaching lush, green pastures? I can see them bursting onto the scene, eagerly grazing the green carpet to satisfy their hunger.

Physical nurture ranks high in our hierarchy of needs. How beautifully the psalmist describes our Lord's intention to meet our need for food: He leads us to the sources that provide nourishment capable of sustaining our bodies.

Later, Jesus illustrates God's nurture by meeting the hunger needs of those who follow him. At the heart of his "Sermon on the Mount," delivered to a crowd among whom were many impoverished and hungry, who, no doubt, were concerned about where their next meal was coming from, Jesus declares:

"...do not be worried about food and drink you need in order to stay alive.... Isn't life worth more than food.... Look at the birds; they do not plant seeds, gather a harvest, and put it in barns; yet your Father in heaven takes care of them! Aren't you worth more than birds" (Matthew 6:25a-26-Today's English Version)?

Not only did Jesus *talk* about nurturing his followers, he *demonstrated* that teaching in his own provision of food for the hungry. Take, for example, that incident when he fed 5,000 of his followers with such abundance that twelve baskets were leftover.

I grew up in a family that always offered a prayer of thanksgiving (or "Grace") before meals. When I became a father, I continued the practice and continue it to this day? Why did my parents think that giving thanks for our meals was an important thing to do? Why do my wife and I? Because, it reminded and reminds us that the ultimate source of our food is God's good grace. That reminder keeps us sensitive to the character of God as that of a good shepherd intent upon making sure that the hunger needs of his flock are met.

Have you experienced the need for the fulfillment we have been describing? Have you ever found your food pantry empty and your pockets "down to your last penny," and felt anxious about whether you were going to have enough for you or your family to eat, when a solution came, perhaps as a care package left at your door or a check in the mail? I've been there! I remember how God came through with the very substance my family and I needed. As I reflect upon it, I recognize such help came through another human being which, I have learned, is the means by which the Good Shepherd meets so many of our needs.

My heart delights when I observe communities like our own here in Sarasota responding to hunger needs around us. Two examples shine like stars on a dark night. First, our "Season of Sharing," a community-wide emphasis upon creating a fund from which expenditures may be made to meet hunger and other critical needs among our citizens who have become victims of various forms of crisis. This past year that effort raised 5.2 million dollars, enabling our community to respond to 3,404 areas of critical need, ranging from provision of food to rent support and Covid-19 relief. A second example is our "All Faiths Food Bank" (AFFB) which targets hunger in our multi county area. In 2020 AFFB distributed 22,430,959 million pounds of food to children, families, seniors and veterans. Of that, 8,113,926 million pounds consisted of fresh produce. Additionally, 18,413,443 million meals were distributed. These figures do not include the contribution of our area's many churches, civic groups and neighborhoods which collect and distribute food directly to the hungry. These are beautiful examples of how God provides for his sheep of many pastures; ensuring that they are physically nourished.

The need for physical nourishment is one aspect of human need. There are others, for a human being is more than *body*. We are also *spirit* and *soul*. In the Hebrew understanding, our bodies and souls are inextricably linked, merged, if you will, so that if one is attended and not the other, both will suffer. Hence, the need to avoid a common delusion that has existed among human kind for centuries, namely, that if we just feed people, they will be fine. Or, if we just attend their spiritual needs, we have fulfilled the limits of our compassion.

Thankfully, in the evolution of our response to human need, benevolent society—particularly the Church—has learned to respond to the whole of human beings—body *and* soul. For example, on mission fields, the church's representatives not only teach religious values and provide instruction regarding their practice, but proceed to provide fresh water wells and agricultural and construction techniques, as well.

Psalm 23 recognizes that our need for nurture is deeper than physical hunger. We also have a need for such fulfilling experiences as times for rest, meditation, and reflection; for those things that restore us in mind and spirit.

Listen to the psalm as it continues: In the second part of verse 2, following the reference to *"green pastures"*, the psalm declares, *"He leads me beside still waters."* I like scholar Mitchell Dahood's translation of this verse: *"Near tranquil waters will he guide me ...."* This is a reference to the tranquility to which our Lord leads us. It is a scene of rest, relaxation, reflection, and peacefulness, widening the scope of the Lord's nurturing care from that of providing the food of green pastures to include the body's *emotional/spiritual* dimension. This seems to be the point of the following verse which affirms: (by such acts *"He restores my soul"* (verse 3—NRSV) or *"...to refresh my being"*—(The Anchor Bible).

I suspect that most of you reading this book are acutely aware of our need for peace of mind and spirit reflected in promises to provide rest and tranquility. It's evident in our wider culture, too. For example, I often hear someone say, "I'm running on fumes" or "I feel worn out, spent, burned out. I need renewal!"

I believe the challenges of modern life are constantly draining us of both physical and spiritual energy with the result that we often feel tired, and emaciated—dispirited and deflated. Do you recall that Jesus himself often felt the need to withdraw from the crowds and seek solace for his mind and spirit in order, effectively, to reengage?

Along with the splendid example of Jesus, we need to recognize the profound (and similar) truth reflected in one of St. Augustine's prayers: "Thou hast made us for Thyself, and our hearts are restless until they find their rest in Thee."

I am not surprised that to the extent that an individual or a society moves away from God, to that extent they will become physically and spiritually exhausted, burning themselves out with a loss of the sense of purpose and meaning.

The writer of Psalm 23 brings good news to such dismay. Having experienced the wide fulfillment of his humanity, the Divine nurture of his whole being, he raises his enthusiastic praise to God, and we have it preserved in this magnificent treasure from the *Psalter*.

For me, this is one of the many precious promises to those who follow the Good Shepherd, that we will be nurtured to health in mind, body and soul, to the point at which life becomes a gift to be celebrated. It is a promise that stands firm, *particularly* when we are facing difficulty and struggle. Take, for example, Psalm 107 in which the writer is praising God for nurturing the faithful precisely in face of extreme difficulty:

"Some were living in gloom and darkness, prisoners suffering in chains, because they had rebelled against the commands of Almighty God and had rejected his instructions. They were worn out from hard work; they would fall down, and no one would help. Then in their trouble they called to the Lord and he saved them from their distress. He brought them out of their gloom and darkness and broke their chains in pieces...He breaks down doors of bronze and smashes iron bars.... Some sailed over the ocean in ships, earning their living on the seas. They saw what the Lord can do, his wonderful acts on the seas. He commanded, and a mighty wind began to blow and stirred up the waves. The ships were lifted high in the air and plunged down into the depths. In such danger the sailors lost their courage; they stumbled and staggered like drunks—all their skill was useless. Then in their trouble they called to the Lord, and he saved them from their distress. He calmed the raging storm, and the waves became quiet. They were glad because of the calm and he brought them safe to the port they wanted. They must thank the Lord for his constant love, for the wonderful things he did for them. They must proclaim his greatness in the assembly of the people and praise him before the council for the leaders" (Psalm 107:10-14,16, 23-32—(TEV).

Now some of you may be thinking that the Psalm 23 represents a rose colored, pollyannish way of thinking that defies reality; particularly in light of the difficulty with which humankind is confronted in destructive forces such as pandemics, national and world chaos, threats of nuclear proliferation and climate degradation.

You may be asking, "Is this promise of sufficient fulfillment of physical and emotional need credible in face of such difficulty? Aren't we caught up in a predicament for which there is no solution? Isn't the combination of world hunger and psychological disintegration going to do us all in?"

I understand, from a mere *rational* perspective, how that thinking may seem appropriate in face of such tremendous odds. Yet, as a person of faith who affirms that the Lord is my shepherd, I hear another drumbeat in the background, that of trust in God's love and sovereignty which calls for a response that includes rationality while, at the same time, transcends its limitations.

I believe Jesus is alluding to this drumbeat when he declares: *"Peace I leave with you; my peace I give you. I do not give to you as the **world** gives. Do not let your hearts be troubled, and do not let them be afraid"* (John 14:27—NRSV). I believe Jesus is calling us to a perspective that, rooted in an affirmation of and trust in *God's sovereignty,* goes to regions that transcend mere reason.

Based on my own experience of God's nurture, I believe, even in the face of difficulty, that God does, indeed, provide for us just *what* we need, *when* we need it, regardless of any confronting difficulty.

While I have not experienced a great number of personal crises to this point in my journey, the few I did experience were powerful, threatening me at multiple levels, including those of job security and emotional stability. During such experiences, there were many sleepless nights as I analyzed the situations, looking for a solution. There were days I was on edge, wondering where the next "attack" would come from.

While I experienced serious anxiety, I prayerfully sought the Lord's peace. In every case that peace eventually came, the dark tunnel through which I had been travelling gave way to the light of its exit. Moreover, as I reflected upon the struggle of the experiences, I always found new strength and fresh peace and was able, again, to cry out in praise to the Good Shepherd's nurture that had "restored my soul."

In his Letter to the Philippians, St. Paul reveals own conviction about God's care that seems so incredible in face of human struggle:

"Rejoice in the Lord, always; again, I will say, rejoice. Let your gentleness be known to everyone. The Lord is near. Do not worry about anything, but, in everything by prayer and supplication with thanksgiving, let your requests be made known to God, And the peace of God *which surpasses all understanding* ('which is far beyond human understanding'—TEV) will guard your hearts and your minds in Christ Jesus" (4:4-7—NRSV).

Oh, yes, the psalmist is onto something very real when he declares: *"The Lord is my shepherd, He makes me lie down in green pastures, he leads me beside quiet waters,* **he restores my soul.***"* Indeed, he is onto something very real and penetratingly relevant to any who are confronted with such seemingly unsurmountable issues.

Profoundly, in face of the threat of non-being, the psalmist declares the restoration of being as the powerful work of the Good Shepherd. I sense that the psalmist, having talked about the physical and emotional nourishment provided by the shepherd, now utilizes a very powerful image—that of soul restoration!

When I hear the power of that imagery, in genuinely fresh ways, I conclude that the nourishing work of the shepherd is so profound that it results in the restoration of our total being as if to declare, "The shepherd recreates us into that which we were before we were threatened by the crises that surround us!"

At this point in the psalm, I sense a slight, but important, transition. Let's proceed to the next chapter to explore that to which the writer is about to expose us.

Insight Exercise for Chapter 1

Insight: Shepherd care comes in the form of NURTURE

Questions to ponder/discuss:

1. How have you experienced God's nurture for your physical being?

2. In what ways have you experienced God's nurture emotionally and spiritually?

3. How has an experience of God's nurturing care affected you?

CHAPTER 2
The Shepherd's *Protective* Care

*"Even though I walk through the darkest valley,
I fear no evil, for you are with me."*

If we stopped our exploration of Psalm 23 at this point, we might be tempted to conclude that the walk of faith is all about receiving the blessings of God's nourishing care and that, therefore, faith's posture has to do with *receiving* as opposed to *giving*. But that is not where the psalmist is coming from. Appropriately in touch with his own faith's insistence that his covenant with God involves both *receiving* and *giving*, he sees faithful living as a combination of dynamic divine and human activity rather than a mere static reception of God's blessings.

So, in verse 3 he moves beyond his symbolic passive scenes of *green pastures* and *quiet* waters to declare, *"He leads me in paths of righteousness"* (NRSV) or, in another translation: *"He leads me in right paths"* (TEV), as though the feeding and resting are intended to strengthen us for *action*, i.e., the journey and the situations to which it will introduce us.

Pause for a moment, now, and sense the dynamic of that transition. From the former scene of the soul restoring result of relaxing in green pastures beside still waters, the flock, now dynamically recharged, is up and moving, continuing its journey. The shepherd is alert to his responsibility to lead the flock onto "right paths" to ensure arrival at their destination. The sheep are sharply responsive to following the shepherd's guidance.

The concept of "right path" is important and deserves some special attention. What does he mean by the term? The psalmist has full awareness that the treacherous terrain through which he must lead his flock demands his closest attention to *right* paths versus *wrong ones*. Following a wrong path could prove disastrous! He knows that right paths—as opposed to wrong ones—are not without threat, to be sure, but they are pathways the shepherd knows well and on which he will be able better to protect the flock from inevitable exposure to dangerous natural phenomena such as wild animals, particularly wolves, and to very dangerous cliffs from which falls could result in severe injury or death. Add to all those dangers the possibility of becoming lost in a wilderness so complex that endless wandering to find one's way is a distinct possibility. Taking the right path is extremely important! That is the challenge of the shepherd's leading.

As we apply this to the journey of faith, what is the deeper meaning of "paths of righteousness" or "right paths"? Answering that correctly constitutes a very strong challenge for modern folk like you and me. Why? In large part because with the passage of time, there has emerged a change in our perception of "right paths" because of the change in our understanding of what our faith—or religion in general--requires of us.

I suspect that many of us reading this book are programmed to think of right paths as making sure we are "towing the line" or "staying on the straight and narrow" through careful attention to a set of "dos" and don'ts." That thinking has its roots in a legalistic or moralistic perception regarding God's expectation of us. The psalmist's perception of right paths is much more profound than such obsession with rules by which to keep oneself in line.

While, no doubt, the psalmist believed in the importance of personal piety, he did not think of it either in legalistic or self-righteous terms. For him—as was the case with many of his Hebrew religiously sophisticated brothers and sisters—the walk of faith placed more emphasis upon one's openness to God and compassion for one's fellow human beings; particularly those who were oppressed by injustice.

In this case, to act with mercy and justice toward others was more prominent in righteous living than whether one went to the field to get an ear of corn to roast on the Sabbath or read material of the same genre as D.H. Lawrence's *Lady Chatterley's Lover*.

Moralistic legalism and its preoccupation with rules and doctrines; particularly as those were later so prevalent among the Pharisees, had not yet developed to the point of such prominence. The faithful lifestyle was still more concerned about practicing reverence for God and acting with justice toward those who had become victims of oppression.

In time, that would change. Within a couple of centuries, a view would emerge which would change our understanding of what it means to be religious. It would lean more in the direction of dogmatism, moralism and legalism as seen in the in the pharisaical legalism with which Jesus had to contend in the first century, a phenomenon that had already occurred a number of times in the history of Israel and would again raise its ugly head in the Christian movement.

In his 1963 book, *The Meaning and End of Religion,* William Cantwell Smith, a professor of comparative religions at Harvard, addressed this change. He detected a critical shift in the way we view the religious life, contending that the former view had come to an end. Smith points out that the end of religion had come, i.e., an end to religion as it has been understood by the noble prophets of Israel. Smith makes the case that this new way of defining religion—in contrast to the former way of the prophets—placed more emphasis upon such issues as believing the right doctrines and following religion's rules for right living and less upon an open heart toward God and compassion toward one's fellow human.

Smith held that "religion" had taken a turn which had changed its original *positive* meaning into something *negative*. He pointed out that the newer definition, which began to emerge prominently as early as the seventeenth century, had begun to perceive religion as a system of *ideas* and *beliefs* about God. He writes:

> In pamphlet after pamphlet, treatise after treatise, decade after decades, the notion was driven home that religion is something that one believes or does not believe, something whose propositions are true or untrue, something whose locus is the realm of the intelligible, is up for inspection before the speculative mind."**1**

More recently, Diana Butler Bass, in her book *Christianity After Religion*, confirms Smith's conclusion regarding this unfortunate change of meaning:

> In modern times, religion became indistinguishable from systematizing *ideas* (italics mine) about God, religious institutions and human beings; it categorized, organized, objectified, and divided people into exclusive worlds of right versus wrong, true versus false, "us" versus "them." **2**

What is their point (Smith and Bass)? To my mind, they are suggesting that in earlier times *religio* (from which we get our English word, "religion") referred to "something in men's (sic) *hearts*" (Smith). However, in modern times religion has morphed into something in men's *minds,* having to do more with doctrines to be believed and rules of behavior to be obeyed than a behavior-modifying attitude toward God and all of life.

In other words, while the earlier focus of religion had been upon nurturing loving relationships with God and with other human beings (things of the heart), the shift we have just described began to perceive religion as focusing upon doctrines and beliefs (things for the mind).

There are inevitable consequences that follow such a shift from *loving behavior to things to be believed* (enough for Smith to see the shift as marking *the end of religion!!*) One consequence that surfaces immediately is a trend toward division, friction, even war, over right doctrines in which loving others becomes replaced with a preoccupation with how to overcome and "convert" others to one's point of view.

With respect to our focus upon Psalm 23, this change on how we view religion and ethics impacts our understanding of right paths, pushing us to view "paths of righteousness" as adopting legalistic rules and moralistic behavior in such a way that love, mercy and justice get minimized or destroyed as our souls yield to an enslaving *works*-righteous (with its cousin, *self*-righteousness), and to poisonous judgmentalism that causes us to condemn those we think are not living up to the standards of a rule book approach to faithful living.

I believe we can accurately say that, when writing about "paths of righteousness" or "right paths," the writer of Psalm 23 had in mind, not so much right doctrines and moralistic ethics, but a lifestyle that expresses itself through loving relationships with God (the shepherd) and with one another (the followers) that compel us to practice love, mercy and justice toward every *one* and *everything* around us.

With the new definition of religion, described by Smith and Bass, that loving relationship dimension fades into the background (or disappears completely) in the frantic effort to determine correct beliefs and moralistic behavior, along with the accompanying tendency to regard others as adversaries to be overcome.

The fallout of this change of emphasis has resulted in additional consequences, for example, in the theological splits earmarked in the prolific denominationalism that followed and the bitterness that grew between Protestants and Catholics and among the hundreds of denominations that emerged to compete with one another (often hatefully) for the minds of people they wanted to win over. And, in other ways as well, for example, as we have already implied, along with this emphasis upon beliefs and doctrines there came a growing belief that being a person of faith demanded rigid behavior (moralism) governed by innumerable rules and prohibitions (legalism), all of which became reflected in a tendency to judge others on the basis of how successful or unsuccessful they became in measuring up to that moralism and legalism (judgementalism).

If this sounds familiar it may be that you are remembering the run-in Jesus had in his counter with Pharisaical legalism in the New Testament (more on this later in this chapter).

Now, back to my conviction that spurred the discussion of the last few paragraphs, the one in which I am contending that the shift from matters of the heart to matters of the mind has made our perception of being led in right paths more difficult than I needs to be. If right paths have to do with establishing loving relationships with God and God's creation, that's one thing. However, if the right paths have to do with a system of beliefs or doctrines, along with rule book prescriptions for correct conduct, that's quite another thing.

That is not to say that there is no role for beliefs, doctrines, and personal piety in living faithfully. It is, however, to declare that maximizing dynamic loving relationships with our God (shepherd) and with all creatures, relationships that insist on trusting God and practicing mercy and justice toward one another, represents the essence of walking the right paths to which the former, wrongly interpreted and applied, can desensitize us.

The relative importance of intellectual beliefs

and living by the "rules," on the one hand, and establishing loving relationships as priorities for faithful living, on the other, is clarified in Jesus' response to Pharisaic legalism.

Let's look more closely at the incident in which Jesus encounters the Pharisees over the issue of what faith requires of us: a lawyer, who is a Pharisee, confronts Jesus with this question: *"Which is commandment in the law is greatest?"* Listen carefully to Jesus' response: *"'You shall love he Lord you God with all your heart and with all your soul, and with all your mind. This is the greatest and first commandment. And a second is like it: 'you shall love your neighbor as yourself.' On these two commandments hang all the law and the prophets"* (Matthew 22:36-40—NRSV).

The Living Bible gives us this paraphrase: *"Love the Lord your God with all your heart, soul, and mind.' This is the first and greatest commandment. The second most important is similar: 'Love your neighbor as much as you love yourself.' All the other commandments and all the demands of the prophets stem from these two laws and are fulfilled if you obey them."* (I discuss this issue more thoroughly in my book, *Journeying Forward Toward Spiritual Freedom* (Workbook Press, 2021).

When we come to realize that walking the right paths has more to do with the action of loving God and God's creation (including other humans) we are rescued from such pitfalls as *moralism* and *legalism* and their complex and confusing mazes. That rescue confronts us with a dynamic challenge. While we may no longer be preoccupied with making sure we have the right doctrine or belief that puts us safely in the *right* path as opposed to the *wrong* path of those who hold different beliefs, and, while we may give up searching the "rule book" to determine correct faithful behavior, we may discover that moving toward and living within loving relationships is not always easy. However, at the same time, we may find, in the process of opening our heart to God and to others, we are provided amazing clarity and deep empowerment with which to develop these loving relationships and, thereby, to live faithfully.

In short, what I am suggesting is this: that following our Shepherd along the "paths of righteousness" has more to do with the heart than the head. Such walk demands of us, not so much mental calculation about right behavior, but a condition of the heart that enables us, in each situation we face, to act in love.

Our task, therefore, becomes that of *discerning* what it means to love God, our fellow human beings, and the entirety of God's creation in all situations.

For me, an important additional challenge is that of *trusting* God's leading (once it has been discerned) in face of any threat, and allowing that trust to generate more love for God and for those around me in the network of creation. For example, do I trust God's leading to get me through complex and critical situations with which contemporary life confronts me? Moreover, does that trust generate the compassion needed to care about others so deeply that, on the one hand, I stretch beyond my comfort zone to meet their need, and, on the other, to risk becoming their advocate if they are trapped in unjust circumstances. Moreover, does that trust in God motivate me to make special effort to conserve this wonderful planet's ecosystem as a gift from God?

Emphasizing trust and love for God and receiving its inspiration to love fellow pilgrims on life's journey, along with the earth on which we travel, constitute a higher calling that is more important to me than haggling over beliefs concerning Moses and the burning bush, whether Methuselah lived for 969 literal years, the appropriate amount of water for baptism, the frequency of celebrating Holy Communion, our perceptions of just how the Scriptures are inspired of God, etc.

In a world society filled with injustice, I believe one of the most "holy" things I can do is to work for the freedom of its victims. Surrounded by thousands who are hungry, to please God and my heart I must advocate for feeding them. Where there are great numbers of fellow human beings caught in the web of political, social and religious oppression, a right path seems always to work toward lifting the heavy yoke that holds them in bondage. In addition, in a religious culture in which a great number of religious persons embrace modes of religious legalism, a right path also demands that we embrace those very legalists with compassion.

The foundation for these convictions regarding the relative importance of beliefs and action, I believe, is laid in our Hebrew heritage and is further confirmed in the Christian movement which followed Jesus' ministry, death, and resurrection. We refer to this combination of traditions as the Judeo-Christian tradition and I suspect that most who read this book stand in, or are familiar with it.

Let's explore briefly the foundation of our conviction that living faithfully has more to do with doing justice and practicing mercy than what beliefs one holds. Let's begin by recalling that, throughout the Old Testament, the prophets of God had a special interest in reminding the Hebrew people that love for God and for God's creation was paramount. In fact, it is significant that Jesus' response to the Pharisee's question about which is the greatest commandment contains two quotes taken from the Old Testament books, *Deuteronomy* and *Leviticus*. For centuries of their history, loving God was held to be the rich soil from which to grow compassion for one another, with a *particular* concern for victims of discrimination, oppression, and neglect. The importance of seeking justice for these victims, was considered to be second only to loving God. Out of ancient Hebrew history Jesus lifts these two commands and, not only calls them the two most important ones, but declares that when we obey the commands to love God and to love our neighbor, we are fulfilling the entire law of God.

The call for honoring God and others with our love is enunciated eloquently, particularly by the 8th century (BCE) prophets. Consider two—Amos and Micah:

AMOS

Responding to the fact that God's people had strayed from the right paths, even while continuing the rituals of worship, Amos exclaimed God's warning and exhortation:

I hate, I despise your festivals, and I take no delight in your solemn assemblies. Even though you offer me your burnt offerings and grain offerings, I will not accept them; and the offerings of well-being of your fatted animals I will not look upon. Take away from me the noise of your songs. I will not listen to the melody of your harps. *But let justice roll down like waters, and righteousness like an ever-flowing stream"* (5:21-24 -NRSV).

The justice to which Amos refers relates to a setting in which human beings get right and good treatment; especially the poor and the stranger; indeed, all who were being marginalized.

For them, justice demands affirming recognition and treatment. So, through Amos, God declares, *"let justice roll down like waters! And righteousness* (the rightness of a loving attitude and loving behavior toward God and one's fellow human beings) *flow like an everlasting stream."*

In short, in the Hebrew context, to be religious—to walk right paths-- is not so much having the right belief or doctrine. It has everything to do with having a relationship with God that becomes an initiator of and a channel for justice and mercy for other people. In other words, to be religious is not so much a matter of the *head*, but of the *heart* and *hands*.

MICAH

The prophet, Micah, making the same point, gives us a message the last words of which have been memorized by millions:

With what shall I come before the Lord, and bow myself before God on high? Shall I come before him with burnt offerings with calves a year old? Will the Lord be pleased with thousands of rams, with ten thousand rivers of oil? Shall I give my firstborn for my transgressions, the fruit of my body for the sins of my soul? No, He (God) has told you, O mortal, what is good; and what does the Lord require of you, but to do justice, and to love kindness, and to walk humbly with your God" (6:6-9-NRSV).

I like Today's English Version's rendering of the last verse: *What he (the Lord) requires of us is this: to do what is just, to show constant love, and to live in humble fellowship with our God.*

When Jesus took upon himself the mantle of "The Good Shepherd," he may very well have had Psalm 23 in mind. Though arriving centuries later, as a faithful Jew, he reflects an understanding of "paths of righteousness" similar to that of the psalmist.

In the setting to which I have already referred, the one in which he is confronting the extreme legalism and moralism of the Pharisees, Jesus cuts through the hundreds of legalistic rules they have established to govern their lives and to make them acceptable to God, to declare a simple but profound insight, namely, that living faithfully—walking the paths of righteousness—is a matter of establishing and honoring loving relationships and, when needed, going to the mat to demand justice for all. Let's read it again:

> When the Pharisees heard that Jesus had silenced the Sadducees, they came together and one of them, a teacher of the Law, tried to trap him with a question. 'Teacher,' he asked, 'which is the greatest commandment of the Law?'
>
> Jesus answered, 'Love the Lord your God with all your heart, with all your soul, and with all your mind.' This is the greatest and the most important commandment. The second most important commandment is like it: 'Love your neighbor as you love yourself.' The whole Law of Moses and the teachings of the prophets depend on these two commandments" (22:34-40-TEV).

Again, as in the case of the prophets, in describing the paths of righteousness, Jesus' emphasis is not upon beliefs or moralistic legalism, rather, it is upon our loving relationship with God and with fellow human beings, the proper nexus for love, kindness, mercy and justice.

I suspect the shift of emphasis from codes and rules to the nature of our relationships must have been somewhat baffling to our Lord's followers then, as now. How does one find her or his way when the rule book, with its "black and white directions," has been removed? I believe Jesus sensed that frustration and was moved to make this promise: "I still have many things to say to you, but you cannot bear them now. When the Spirit of truth comes, *he will guide you into all the truth....* (John 16:12-13a-NRSV).

In my experience the right path (the path of righteousness) is not always crystal clear. There are morally ambiguous issues and situations that demand more of us than turning to page 399, rule number 35, in our morality rulebook for the answer. Rather, we are sent to our knees in prayer, seeking to discern the right thing to do. For example, you may remember Adolph Hitler's determination to destroy all Jews--he called it the "Final Solution". Stories abound, telling how numerous people of conscience invited those threatened into their homes, hiding them in their attics in order to avoid the Nazi soldiers who would come knocking at the door and inquiring about whether they were entertaining any Jewish guests. These incidents confronted the hosts with the dilemma of telling the truth, thus surrendering their guests to the Nazis, or lying to protect them. These brave hosts would answer, "No! No Jews here!"

When those protectors of precious lives weighed the various moral dimensions of their dilemma, they opted to lie.... in order to serve a purpose with greater moral implications, namely, that of saving the lives of her Jewish neighbors.

Do we not face similar issues that defy rule-book simplicity—whether to abort a fetus with diagnosed physical and/or mental difficulties, whether to support "illegal aliens" who are among us, whether to lend support to someone who believes he or she is gay, whether to withhold life-support from someone, in a vegetative state, without a living will? These are just a few of the issues we face, all of which defy the naiveté of the rule-book approach to morality.

In face of such ambiguity, what is a person of faith to do? Are we left without guidance? I believe the promise Jesus made, as recorded in John 16, is that the Holy Spirit will *guide* us onto the right path if we posture ourselves for discernment. (For a moment, ponder the thought that, even after Jesus' ascension into heaven, we continue to be shepherded through the guiding influence of the Holy Spirit!!)

Admittedly, not everyone will discern the Spirit's guidance in the same way. Some may feel led left while others are led right. Such a scenario demands of us a tolerant spirit that enables us to affirm those who have perceived guidance differently. I believe such tolerance is able to deliver us from the all-too-frequent tendency to reject those who have come to a different conclusion about the right path. The practice of such tolerance demands that we accept diversity—even moral diversity—in our communities, trusting that such loving tolerance finds favor with our Good Shepherd who spoke so eloquently of our love for God and for one another.

Following that excursion, let's now get back, directly, to Psalm 23. We have discussed how in verses 1-2, he describes our relationship with the shepherd as one that not only feeds us *physically* and sustains us *emotionally* and *spiritually*, with the result that we are renewed and restored. Also, we have seen that he views that relationship as one in which the shepherd leads us into action (verse3b), specifically, walking "right paths," understood as actively loving God with all our hearts, and actively loving our fellow human beings with such depths that we are willing to go to bat for them that they may receive justice.

Now, let us notice that he concludes verse three by declaring that the shepherd leads us onto right paths *for his name's sake*. That is an important ending to the verse in that it emphasizes that the character of God is honored when we follow God onto paths of righteousness. In other words, leading us onto paths of righteousness proves that God is credible and trustworthy and our willingness to follow upon those paths is proof that we honor God's character.

In his 2 Corinthian letter, St. Paul affirms this insight in another way, through the image of God's followers as "letters."

This is his declaration:

Could it be, like some other people, we need letters of recommendation to you or from you? You yourselves are the letter we have, written on our hearts for everyone to know and read. It is clear that Christ himself wrote this letter and sent it by us. It is written, not with ink but with the Spirit of the living God, and not on stone tablets but on human hearts" (3:1b-3).

Believers in the Corinthian congregations are being reminded that they are perceived in the general public as letters of recommendation from both God and the apostle. I think the Corinthian passage, when laid parallel to the psalmist's statement, "He leads us in paths of righteousness *for his name's sake,"* raises at least these two questions for us: Does your letter (i.e., your life of faith) recommend God to those around you? Are you experiencing fulfillment in the promise of God to bring right and good things to you and to others as a result of God's leading you onto the right paths?

I believe this is a portion of the point of the psalmist's comment: "He leads me in paths of righteousness *for his name's sake"* (23:3). In other words, because our behavior reflects the character of God, let us behave in a way that honors the name and character of God, resulting in an experience of the fulfillment of God's promise to bless us.

This chapter's title alludes to the Shepherd's *protective* care. Let's move ahead with that theme by acknowledging that the psalmist's native country is marked with considerable wilderness often consisting of treacherous and steep mountains and innumerable rocks and crevices.

Upon my first visit to the country of Israel in 1998, with others in my tour group, I entered from the country of Jordan. After crossing the Jordan River, the first village we came upon was the Palestinian town of Jericho which is overshadowed by the Mt. of Temptation, a high and treacherous looking peak that rises out of the Jordan Valley, piercing the sky and towering over the town and its surrounding areas.

Upon viewing the mountain from the valley, I was deeply impressed by its majesty and mystery, my imagination, perhaps, enhanced by the dramatic story of our Lord's temptation there. You may remember that Satan's temptations came in three forms: the temptation to turn stones into bread in order to be fed, the temptation to worship the devil in order to be made ruler of the entire world and the temptation to cast himself from the temple heights, to be parachuted safely to the ground by God's angels and, thereby, achieve instant notoriety.

As my view of the mountain widened, I noticed how treacherous was the surrounding terrain with its deep valleys, multitudinous numbers of rocks in all sizes, and the stark landscape. Later, upon leaving Jericho by way of the "road up to

Jerusalem," I felt a chill as I viewed the amazing depth of the valley that lay just north of that road.

Following our visit to the interior of Israel, we explored the areas containing the caves of the now famous Dead Sea Scrolls, Masada, and the Dead Sea itself. Leaving the area, on our return to Jordan, we visited Petra and the surrounding remains of the ancient Nabatean civilization with their distinct dwellings carved out of the great mounds of sandstone. From that experience, I remember coming away with the deep impression that, while the Middle East was so important—and in many ways—beautiful, it was abundant with treacherous wilderness areas filled with potential for natural calamity for any who travel there.

All this is to underscore the significance of the psalmist's declaration that his shepherd leads him in right paths, paths surrounded by danger which by their very nature demanded the guidance and protection of an experienced and trustworthy shepherd.

So, the psalmist now moves into the heart of the journey's danger, admitting that it contains a *"valley of the shadow of death"* (KJV) or *"darkest valley"* (NRSV), or valley of *"deepest darkness"* (TEV). In face of its threat, he declares, *"Even though I walk through the darkest valley, I fear no evil, for you are with me; your rod and your staff—they comfort me"* (23:4).

Here the psalmist is giving us some strong stuff:

To be led by our shepherding God does not mean we will not face the dangers of life. Jesus' own life faced multiple struggles ranging from hunger to rejection; from loneliness to physical abuse, and the like. Life is full of uncertainties. Humans are vulnerable to disease and deprivation. But it is precisely those conditions that require a good shepherd, one who will lead us *through*; one in whom we place our trust, enabling us to complete the journey successfully.

Do you catch a precious insight about the nature of faith here? To be a faithful follower does not guarantee that we will not be *affected* by life's difficulties, it's promise is that we will not be *defeated* by them.

This insight is made clear in a Face Book post I received from a former parishioner that she had received from a source calling itself Ozark Revival and dated January 6, 2021:

Faith doesn't always take you out of the problem. Faith takes you through the problem.

Faith doesn't always take away the pain. Faith gives you the ability to handle the pain.

Faith doesn't always take you out of the storm. Faith calms you in the midst of the storm

Perhaps, as I am, you are impressed by the difference in translations when it comes to describing the valley. The King James Version (KJV) on which so many of us were reared renders it: *"...though the valley of the shadow of death...."* But others, including the much-trusted New Revised Standard Version (NRSV) offers, *"...through the darkest valley....'*

The KJV links the valley to that overshadowed by death which has led millions down through the ages to find solace in the dying experience. For example, I remember when a faithful member of my congregation was actively dying the family had gathered around her bed and requested that I repeat Psalm 23. As I quoted it in the KJV, when we came to the words, *"Even though I walk through the valley of the shadow of death, I fear no evil...,"* a special feeling seemed to come over us all, a strong sense of God's presence, there to deliver her to the other side but, at the same time, tenderly to care for the family to whom she was important.

At another time and place, I remember my friend (Paul) whom I visited in the hospital. As I walked into his room, I noticed a despondent look on his face. "How're you doing?" I asked. He winced and responded, "Not very well, Jim, I'm in bad shape and my doctor wants me to have more surgery.

"How do you feel about his plan for surgical treatment?"

"I'm both hurt and angry," he responded. "I'm dying, and quite O.K with it, but the doctor wants me to have surgery which, to me, means we're just needlessly prolonging the struggle that I've finally come to grips with."

After thinking for a moment, I said to him, "Have you considered letting your doctor know how you feel about the situation? I find doctors to be pretty understanding of their patients' wishes."

After a prayer together, my friend indicated he would consider having that conversation. As I departed, I said to him, "I'll see you tomorrow."

Next afternoon I returned to see him and was met with smiles and evidence of deep relief. "How are you doing today?" I asked.

"Terrific!" he responded. "I talked with my doctor and he seemed to understand completely my desire not to have more surgery. He granted that surgery would not greatly enhance the quality of my life nor extend my longevity considerably, and that he understood my reluctance to do it."

You seem at peace with your decision," I said.

"You bet!" he responded. I think I will sleep well tonight.

It seemed appropriate for us to say together Psalm 23. When we came to *"Even though I walk through the valley of the shadow of death, I will fear no evil for Thou art with me..."* there seemed to be a special and reverent sacredness in the air.

A few days later, my friend died.

Now look at the NRSV rendering of this verse, Here, *"...through the valley of the shadow of death...."* gets translated *"...through the darkest valley...."* This translation widens the scope of God's sovereign care beyond the experience and implications of death to include any life situation that is especially dark and heavy. And of these, there are many. As I write, we are in the midst of a Covid-19 pandemic that has inflicted millions with disease and death. In addition, it has afflicted humankind with everything from economic hardship to social isolation, along with situations that have allowed psychological depression and opportunities for devastating diseases like cancer and heart disease to gallop unchecked as they remain undetected. To so many persons caught in such darkness Psalm 23 has proved to be a Godsend.

I identify with this rendering of the verse in a very personal way. Two years ago, I suffered a heart attack. Its aftermath was very heavy for me. While I had sailed through the attack and treatment episodes rather easily, shortly thereafter, I entered into a period of insomnia, anxiety, and mild depression. My physician prescribed medication for both the insomnia and anxiety which, after a while, enabled me to sleep better and longer. In addition, I began a regiment of spiritual therapy which included a careful recitation (praying) of Psalm 23 just after evening prayers and before sleep. The practice included quoting a phrase of the psalm; then pausing to contemplate its meaning, e.g., ...*green pastures* (pause), ...*still waters*... (pause), etc.

Over time, I began to sleep more soundly; to be less anxious and depressed. As a result, I began (with my doctor's counsel) to wean myself from anxiety medications until I was free from them but I have continued with my spiritual therapy of "praying" the psalm which has brought a new level of physical, emotional, and spiritual stability to my life.

The *key* element in my recovery, to this point, seems to be my spiritual therapy; particularly, dwelling upon the insightful power of the various phrases of Psalm 23 whose *green pastures, quiet waters, restoration of soul, the darkest valley,* coupled with *I will fear no evil, for You are with me...,* along with *goodness and mercy will follow me all the days of my life and I will dwell in the house of the Lord forever* wrap me in their arms of security and carry me to a new level of safety and quality.

I love to combine the two different translations: *Yea though I walk through the valley of the shadow of death...* and *Even though I walk through the darkest valley....* I know the original language of the text is more accurately rendered... *through the darkest valley...(calmuth)* in contrast to... through the valley of the shadow of death... *(cal maweth)* but, taken together, they supply an assurance that both, the valleys of our daily living *and* of our dying will be accompanied by our Good Shepherd who walks beside us all the way through to the other side of the valley.

Because the Good Shepherd is there with us, we ... *fear no evil* (verse 4a-NRSV). Is the psalmist suggesting that our journey through life's dark valleys will be a snap, that there will be no anxiety as we take it all in stride? My own experience leads me to respond, "No!" I have known angst in the experience but the *angst* did not result in a *fearful despair* capable of destroying me. My own sense of the psalmist's meaning, therefore, is that, because of the Shepherd's presence, he will not lose trust and hope because of the confidence he has in the Shepherd's comforting protection.

From there, the psalmist moves on to describe the forms in which that protection comes: *...your rod and staff—they comfort me* (v.4b-NRSV). The comforting protection that sustains the person of faith during the valley struggle is symbolized in both figures—the rod and the staff. The rod, a sharp-pointed instrument used by shepherds to poke at beasts who dared attack the sheep and the staff whose crook was applied gently to the sheep's back both to guide it and to assure it of the shepherd's presence.

How appropriate the symbolism is for the Good Shepherd's relationship to faithful followers who are attacked by hostile forces both seen and unseen, both physical and spiritual, against whom the Good Shepherd uses the rod of protection as a deterrent to their aggression. Have you not experienced such comforting protection from the Lord when you sensed threats from hostile forces, whether they came in form of disease, anger, hatred, discrimination, temptation, injustice, etc.? On the other hand, have you not felt the Shepherd's *staff* gently applied to your spirit; and strengthening your sense of security while, at the same time, correcting and guiding you as you approach and enter a danger zone?

The psalmist is declaring that, because God is with him, guiding, protecting, and assuring, he will not be overcome with paralyzing fear, even when the threat is severe; that hope, love, and trust will assure stability and forward movement, freedom and victory.

From here, he psalmist now takes us into very meaningful territory for faithful persons who are experiencing life's serious threats. He does this by depicting a surrounding enemy whose aggressive behavior is unable to penetrate the shield of protection provided by the shepherd. Not the sheep, but the enemy is pictured as victim which, now, must watch as God dramatically underscores the precious esteem in which God holds those who faithfully follow:

You prepare a table before me in the presence of my enemies; you anoint my head with oil; my cup overflow (verse 6--NRSV).

This verse highlights a cultural practice in the psalmist's religious tradition, namely, recognizing the dignity of the refugee. For example, the man who is hunted by enemies needs only to touch the tent of the one with whom he seeks refuge in order to be safe and enjoy gracious hospitality. His enemies may stand and glare outside the tent door, but can do no more.

Under the Good Shepherd's protective care, the person of faith may experience the pursuit and feel the heat of the enemy's breath, but the Divine Host stops the aggressor, making it watch as the Shepherd prepares and serves a banquet, as if to declare, "While you see him as someone to be abused, even destroyed, I see and protect the value my sons and daughters and celebrate with them!"

Stand back and imagine the scene. The faithful have come through a long journey on paths of righteousness that, at times, have led them through the valley of the shadow of death, a shadow that often accompanies one's faithful advocacy of mercy and justice for marginalized victims. Now the day's journey has ended with a celebration of victory over the danger. Tomorrow will bring a continuation of the vulnerable journey, along with a continuation of God's shepherding care and at its end, another celebration. The day in and day out cycle for the faithful is one of constant struggle accompanied with constant victory and celebration.

Adding to the attractiveness of faithful living, the psalmist alludes to another component in the East's practice of shepherding—a glorious massage from the hands of the Good Shepherd: ...*you anoint my head with oil* (NRSV). While that imagery does not mean a lot to us, in the practice of the ancient near east, it was a means of refreshment for weary travelers, and healing oils were sometimes rubbed into the fleece of sheep. The point seems to be that the Good Shepherd goes the "second mile" in giving renewing power and providing comfort; all as the enemies watch.

This can be the experience of people of faith in all generations—at day's end, delivered from the hands of the enemy to be refreshed and renewed from weariness, restored for blessed continuation. No wonder, then, that the psalmist declares, ...*my cup overflows.*

Contemplate this: at the end of the day's perilous journey, the faithful are able to experience the *abundant* life. In the imagery of that longstanding conundrum of determining whether our glass as half empty or half full, the psalmist is raising this remarkable insight: Following the Good Shepherd through even the valley of death leaves one, at the end of the day, able to exclaim: ...*my cup overflows*—(NRSV)or ... (is filled) ... *to the brim*—(TEV); neither half *empty* or half *full*, but filled completely ... to *the brim!!!*

When, in face of life's enemies, one is able to

experience the shepherd's sumptuous banquet, soothing massage, and overwhelming protection; all while the enemy can only watch, he/she is truly blessed beyond measure and moved to express thanksgiving. That's the message the psalmist provides for us who struggle in our daily lives.

Profoundly, however, this message, like the periscope of a submarine engulfed and surrounded by water, raises its capacity to see beyond the immediate day, our tomorrows, all the way to the ultimate future when the shepherd has led us to our final destination.

Insight Exercise for Chapter 2

Insight: Shepherd care comes in the form of PROTECTION.

Questions to ponder/discuss

1. A component of shepherd protection is the shepherd's leading us onto "paths of righteousness" or "right paths". What is your understanding/experience of these paths?

2. In what ways have you experienced God's protection?

3. Does God's protection insulate you against struggle? Explain:

CHAPTER 3
The Shepherd's Victorious Care

"...and I shall dwell in the house of the Lord my whole life long."

Regarding the tomorrows beyond today, the faithful are able to exclaim, *Surely goodness and mercy shall follow me all the days of my life...* (vs. 6—NRSV). In other words, the psalmist seems to be saying, "That which I have experienced in this sumptuous banquet and this soothing massage (all while my enemy is watching in anxious envy); that I can count on for the remainder of my life."

While nowhere in the psalm is there any mention of the shepherd's dogs, I am aware that, in sheep country, dogs do a great deal in terms of shepherding sheep. Their owners hold the shepherding dogs in high honor. They are aware of their amazing skill and demanding work and how, at the end of the day, not only is a sheep dog exhausted but his wounded and, sometimes, bleeding feet show the extent and effectiveness of his work as a result of which not a single sheep has been lost.

In light of this, a poetic preacher, speaking in the vernacular in order to add force and tenderness to his words, exclaimed, "the Lord is my shepherd, aye, and more than that, he had two fine collie dogs, Goodness and Mercy. With him before and them behind, even poor sinners like you and me can hope to win home at last!"

Dwell on that for a moment: As long as we live, safe between the Good Shepherd who leads up front and the forces of goodness and mercy following behind, we will experience a magnificent sense of security, whatever comes our way!

I think it is this sense of security as we journey faithfully in this present world that Jesus had in mind when he declared: *"I am telling you the truth: those who hear my words and believe in him who sent me have eternal life. They will not be judged, but have **already** passed from death to life"* (John 5:24—TEV).

Here, Jesus is declaring that the faithful have already passed into life, even while in our present bodies of flesh and blood. In other words, we already have one foot in heaven, even before dying and going on to glory where our total being will be immersed into a state of *glorification.*

When I lay Jesus' insight alongside the psalmist's declaration that *Surely, goodness and mercy shall follow me all the days of my life...,* I am led to believe that the psalmist—who lived in a day before the people of Israel had developed a concept of *Heaven—may,* nevertheless, have been experiencing a taste of it.

When Jesus arrives, centuries later, he is clear not only about Heaven but also about the fact that persons of faith have *already entered* it while on their journey with the Good Shepherd and prior to their death.

In the first century, our Lord's disciples experienced a remarkable transformation from considering themselves to be victims of life to experiencing a profound sense of eternal security that was strong and sure. In our own time, we who follow the Lord may experience that same quality of security that enables us to voice our excitement in such expressions as these: "Come hell or high water, I am safe in the arms of God!" "I may not know what tomorrow holds, but I know who holds tomorrow, God, who is greater than any force in the universe!"

It's that the quality of security to which Jesus refers when he declares:

"My sheep hear my voice. I know them and they follow me. I give them eternal life and they will never perish. No one will snatch them out of my hand. What the Father has given me is greater than all else. And no one can snatch it out of the Father's hand. The Father and I are one" (John 10:27-30—NRSV).

Led by our Good Shepherd, we don't have to be paralyzed by fear of threatening forces. Rather, realizing that *the one who is in us greater than the one who is in the world* (I John 4:4—NRSV), we are empowered to move ahead and through the threat, led by the Good Shepherd along *right paths*.

From his vantage point, the psalmist casts his eyes upon the future as though to say, "I've shared a vision of what the faithful walk looks like here and now, but what about the future?" Then, he invites us into the future-focused vision: *and I shall dwell in the house of the Lord my whole life long* (vs. 6b-NRSV).

On hearing that, some may be inclined to complain that this translation lacks the punch of the old King James Version which offers the following: ...*and I shall dwell in the house of the Lord forever.*

Why the difference in translation?

In the first case the psalmist's vision for dwelling in the house of the Lord is limited to his present lifespan, while, on the other, that dwelling is extended beyond this present life into endless existence.

To the extent we are surprised by the difference, we can credit it to the probability that most of us are familiar with King James Version of this psalm. I can hear it now, "I'm a little disappointed for I've always read the psalm to end with an extension of the dwelling in the house of the Lord *forever*; not for just my life time."

I sense it is important, therefore, to address what I understand to be the reason for the difference in the translations:

First, at the time the psalm is written and, given the probability that it is composed by a person who lacks the fuller concept of the afterlife that develops later, the writer is articulating his natural conclusion that the extent of his living is limited to the span of his physical days; that when death comes, so does his experience of conscious companionship with God, the Shepherd. As earlier stated, it is with the advent of Jesus and the subsequent birth and development of the Church and Christian theology that we begin to realize a strong focus upon the concept of Heaven as an experience of our *everlasting* companionship with God.

Recognition of this historical note regarding a *developing* understanding of eternal existence with God, enables us to transition to the *second* reason for the difference in the translations.

While I am not equipped to trace the details of the process leading to a concept of a continuing relationship with God following our physical deaths (Heaven), I do know that the concept develops and grows more clearly following the ministry of Jesus and the experience of the early Church. You may remember the occasion, just before his leaving to return to the Father, on which Jesus declares:

"Do not be worried and upset.... Believe in God and believe also in me. There are many rooms in my Father's house, and I am going to prepare a place for you. I would not tell you this if it were not so. And after I go and prepare a place for you, I will come back and take you to myself, so that you will be where I am" (John 14:1-3—TEV).

The reference to ...*my Father's house* is very close to the last verse of the psalm in which the writer declares, ...*and I shall dwell in the house of the Lord*.... I see here an implication that, in the thinking of Jesus, the *house of the Lord* concept has expanded considerably beyond the physical Temple in Jerusalem and now refers directly to entire domain and being of God. If that is the case, the destiny of those who follow the Good Shepherd's leading is nothing less than that of reaching our destination in eternal fellowship with God.

For example, earlier in this same Gospel (John 10), Jesus described himself as the Good Shepherd, perhaps considering himself as the inheritor of Psalm 23's shepherd image. Thereafter, Jesus' disciples begin to affirm that in his role as our Good Shepherd, Jesus leads us from this life to another, namely, Heaven construed as an experience that transcends our earthly span both in terms of time and quality. * Therefore, the journey on which the Shepherd leads us, does not end with our physical death. It continues toward its *ultimate* destination, namely, eternal life, in direct presence and fellowship, not only with God, but with all creation—including loved ones—now restored in eternal community.

*I remind the reader that this emphasis upon Heaven is not to be construed as a diminishment of the work we are called and empowered to do as we travel through this earthly existence, the work of practicing love for God and for all our fellow human beings as expressed in commitment to justice and mercy. Moreover, be reminded that, in Judeo-Christian thinking, Heaven is the ultimate experience of perfect justice and mercy of which our earthly journey is a foretaste.

I suspect that when the translators of scripture who gave us the King James Version of Psalm 23, came upon this psalm, they did not hesitate to yield a more elaborate rendering of the 23:6. Rather than to translate it, literally, to read, "...as long as I live," or "...the extent of my days," they reflected the influence of the later perspective, choosing to render it, "...forever."

In his scholarly "exposition" on this portion of Psalm 23 in *The Interpreter's Bible*, J.R.P Sclater affirms the role of inspiration in interpreting the psalmist's work:

No doubt the original writer throughout had in his mind solely the protection of God in the vicissitudes of this mortal life. 'I shall have my good days and my bad, but my Lord will see me through the latter, and I shall be able as long as I live to join the worship of his temple.' *The house of the Lord* figured for him the actual temple on the hill. But it is quite impossible for us to interpret the psalm in so restricted a sense. The Lord has touched it with his finger, and enlarged its horizons. Indeed, part of his shepherding of us is precisely the deepening and widening of such a song as this. Wherefore let it be interpreted in the light of our knowledge of him. **1**

From our Christian perspective, both the identity of the psalm's "shepherd" and the nature of our destination are considerably enriched. The *shepherd* becomes Jesus and the destination of the journey on which he leads us is not limited to the end of our physical existence, but extends beyond, to eternal glory with God.

But more needs to be said at this point: I think it is important to recognize that this *heavenly* destination is not some ethereal, bodyless experience somewhere in outer space. Rather, it is existence within a new *incorruptible* (imperishable) body (1 Corinthians 15:50-57) in the midst of the *new heaven and the new earth* (Revelation 21:1-8) that have been enjoined; thus, fulfilling Jesus' prayer, *...Thy kingdom come, thy will be done, on earth as in heaven...* (Matthew 6:10).

This *eternal* destination leads to an experience, not only of restoration of all creation, but to a society reflecting perfect love, justice, and peace under the reign of God.

No wonder Psalm 23 has been given such a prominent place among other expressions of great literature. It has the potential to turn any of the world's aimlessness and purposelessness to a clear journey on right paths, leading all the way to our eternal goal in the Kingdom of God.

It has been my pastoral privilege to take a position by the side of many dying parishioners, holding their hand as they finished their earthly journey. Frequently, these are folk with whom I have already journeyed for a while, keeping in view the positive nature of the journey's end, not as a morbid yielding of ourselves to a grim reaper's scythe, but as an arrival at the gates of our destiny, there to feel the embrace of our loving Creator who, having been with us through the journey, now *lifts* us to new heights of glory and to a quality of eternal fellowship that defies description.

After I wrote that last sentence, taking a break to breath in the glory of the victory to which our Lord "lifts" us, the words of a hymn written by the Reverend Johnson Oatman, Jr. which, as a child and youth, I sang with my home church, came bubbling from its deep recesses to the surface of my mind:

I'm pressing on the upward way. New heights I'm gaining every day.
still praying as I onward go, "Lord plant my feet on higher ground."
Lord, lift me up and let me stand by faith on Heaven's tableland.
A higher plane than I have found; Lord, plant my feet on higher ground."

Some of the most precious moments of my ministry have been those when I sat beside a faithful person in the throes of dying and, from their lips, heard the words,

"I am going home!" Or, sometimes, just the single word "home."

Recently a friend of mine, Doris Heaton of Banner Elk, North Carolina, posted a prayer on Face Book that captures the trusting prayer and expectation of the psalm:

James Bailiff

"Walk with me Father,

until my journey is through.

then, by your grace, bring me home

to You."

Insight Exercise for Chapter 3

Insight: Shepherd care is designed to lead us to
VICTORY

Questions to ponder/discuss

1. What does the victory to which our shepherd leads us mean to you?

2. How have you experienced this victory here in the midst of this life?

3. This victory is designed to extend beyond our earthly span of life. What does that mean to you?

CONCLUSION

The nature of God has been discussed, written and preached about in the form of thousands of images ranging from highly philosophic terms like those of Paul Tillich who described God as "The Ground of Being" to Hollywood's more colloquial "The Man Upstairs." I have heard other image-packed references such as "The Big Guy," The Boss," "The Ultimate," etc. Of all the several images, perhaps the most meaningful to me are those of Psalm 23 and John 10— "Shepherd" or "Good Shepherd."

In rural North Carolina I grew up among animals— pigs, cows, horses—and became close to them as I cared for them through feeding, grooming, and, yes, conversation. With particular affection, I remember our milk cow, Patsy. Not only did I milk her every day, but summer and winter, fed her. On those warm sunny Carolina days, when I came home from school, I would go to her as she lay in the meadow chewing her cud, lie down beside her and, with my head propped up on her abdomen, do my reading assignments with a deep sense of peace and unity. While she never responded to my comments or questions with verbal words, there was certain and affectionate communication. I am quite sure we enjoyed each other's company.

While we had no sheep with whom shepherds are most associated, I loved Patsy as well as our other animals and went to great lengths to make sure they were well cared for. I suspect that is one of the reasons I am so moved by the image of shepherd, hearing and feeling in it the same quality and bond of affection and mutual commitment.

That attraction to the shepherd imagery goes well beyond me, however. For centuries, it has spoken to the hearts of millions, evoking positive feelings. Perhaps that is why the image is so much a part of the biblical tradition as illustrated in Psalm 23 and in Jesus' adoption of the imagery of the Good Shepherd for his own ministry.

As we have discussed the Shepherd's care in these passages, I hope you have experienced, along with me, that special care—exemplified in the psalm's shepherd and exhibited so clearly in the ministry of Jesus—with which people of faith are always surrounded. Never does a day go by when I don't experience the loving care of our Good Shepherd who nurtures me physically and emotionally with the result that I have a sense of security even while I am surrounded by a raging Covid-19 pandemic, disturbing social chaos, and the seduction of a culture that offers us so many wrong paths to successful living.

Daily, one of my most fulfilling moments is that one, following my evening prayers, when I let the words of Psalm 23 come pouring into my mind and spirit. When I have heard the whole of the psalm, I am able to yield to restful sleep, refreshed in an experience of the Lord's tender care.

If you are having undue and lasting anxiety in your own life and if you are having difficulty going to sleep or returning to sleep after waking up, I recommend that you memorize the psalm in order to repeat it as a door leading to peace and tranquility. Your experience will confirm for you that there is power in the psalm to calm and give meaning to your body and spirit.

Some of you are acquainted with *Halley's Bible Handbook*, composed by the Reverend Dr. Henry H. Halley. I have carried it in my pastoral tool box since the beginning, and continue to utilize its information and inspiration. It is loaded with information about the Bible and has continued to be a best seller through the years, selling more than five million copies in many languages.

Commenting on Psalm 23, Dr Halley writes:

Best loved chapter of the Old Testament. Beecher said something like this: 'The Psalm has flown like a bird up and down the earth, singing the Sweetest Song Ever Heard. It has charmed more griefs than all the philosophies of the world. It will go on singing to your children, and to my children, and to their children, till the end of time. And when its work is done, it will fly back to the bosom of God, fold its wings, and sing on forever in the happy chorus of those it had helped to bring there. **2**

If you are now, continue listening to the psalm's music; if not currently listening, turn your spiritual radio on and be renewed in mind and spirit, from head to toe.

Sincerely, I hope you have gleaned something

from this discussion of blessings that come from our focus upon shepherding as that comes to us through the psalmist and through Jesus., the Good Shepherd. It was a joy to write about the blessings. I want you to know how honored I am that you have taken the time to share it with me through the reading of *Shepherd Blessings*. It is my hope that you will experience the good things that come from following God's leading, trusting in the promise inherent in Jesus' declaration: *...I came that they may have life, and have it abundantly* (John 10:10—NRSV).

I leave you with this inspirational picture from Isaiah:

He will feed his flock like a shepherd,

He will gather the lambs in his arms,

And carry them in his bosom,

And gently lead the mother sheep.

(40:11—N.R.S. V.)

END

NOTES

Chapter One

1. Richard J. Foster and Gayle D. Beebe, Longing for God (Downers Grove, Illinois: IVB Books, 20009) p 62

2. Ibid, pp 67-68

3. Mitchell Dahood, The Anchor Bible Commentary (New York: Doubleday and Company 1966) p 145

Chapter Two

1. Winfred Cantwell Smith, The Meaning and End of Religion (New York: Macmillan, 1963) p. 58

2. Diana Butler Bass, Christianity After Religion (New York: Harper One, 2012) p .59

Chapter Three

1. JRP Sclater, "Exposition on Psalm 23," Interpreter's Bible, volume 4 (New York and Nashville: 1955) p. 129

2. Henry H. Halley, Halley's Bible Handbook (Grand Rapids: Zondervan, 1965) p. 255

www.ingramcontent.com/pod-product-compliance
Lightning Source LLC
Chambersburg PA
CBHW021430070526
44577CB00001B/153